To the Intellect of the Wise and the Comforter of Hearts

So Much Love

POEMS BY CHRISTINE BELL

So Much Love

Poems by Christine Bell

First Edition 2006

ISBN 1 - 886872 - 36 - 8

Published by Brahma Kumaris Information Services Ltd
in association with Brahma Kumaris World Spiritual University (UK),
Registered Charity No. 269971.

Global Co-operation House, 65 Pound Lane, London NW10 2HH, UK

www.bkpublications.com
Email: enquiries@bkpublications.com

Printed in India by Srinivas Fine Arts (P) Ltd.,

So Much Love

POEMS BY CHRISTINE BELL

BK PUBLICATIONS

an imprint of

BRAHMA KUMARIS INFORMATION SERVICES LTD., LONDON

Contents

4: Occasions

5: Celebrating Lives

6: Virtue

Foreword

Universally known for their peaceful values and silent meditation, perhaps the Brahma Kumaris family are less commonly appreciated for their sense of occasion and capacity to celebrate. Diwali, Christmas, Shivratri, the dedication of a building, the visit of a much-loved senior yogi, the passing of an old friend... all provide an opportunity for BKs to get together and contribute their own brand of joy and respect. Feelings may be intense as sweet memories are recalled, and those present are often moved or inspired by the experience.

At many of these landmark events, one long-time meditator and member of the BK family, Christine Bell, has been there to capture the moment in a poem. Her perceptive observation of the scene, the insight she brings to what she sees, and her ability to encapsulate emotions and revelations experienced by many give her work a unique quality.

People, places, memorable occasions, and some powerful personal moments are conveyed in these verses.

After these unforgettable events, Christine often reads her poems aloud with such feeling that those who were present can relive their experience, while those who were absent can feel that they have shared in the moment.

This volume will give many of us the chance to rejoice once more in those times of family celebration, to recall memorable places and people and to remember again the still moments, all set down for us by our modest laureate, Christine Bell.

Sister Jayanti

So much love!

Our Dadis
Carry it in their eyes
It sustains them still
And ceaselessly flowing out
Encompasses all of us

I glimpsed BapDada holding them
Circle of subtle light, special foundation souls
Exclusive few yet not excluding me
A total love for true friends
Tempered like steel over time

Love like water, flowing into the
dry ground of my being
Softening the brittle surface
Reviving, refreshing, renewing

Allowing my tenderness to blossom
This love between us was bonded at birth
A mother's love without which
I am powerless, unable to flourish and thrive
It fills me with the certainty of my own goodness
And my capacity to reciprocate love

Your love is in the music
and magic of the murli
My worldly father would write
a weekly letter while I was away

I am so fortunate a child
Receiving now a daily letter of love
from my Father/Teacher
Let me absorb this knowledge so deeply
that it flushes out all my sorrow

Our love requires me to
maintain Your honour

Think, say, do only that
which becomes a true heir
For you have bequeathed
all Your property to me
Brought the gift of a golden land
On the palm of Your hand

Trusted, loving Friend
Touching my deeply felt need
to play and sing and share
the secrets of my heart

Your love is like a fortress
No enemy dare invade
Unless in careless moment
I leave a side gate open
Allow the spy to slip through

Losing heart, strange expression!
Myself and Maya are only too familiar
with this phenomenon
Happily Baba safeguards my heart
Until I claim it back

Is there a lost property store
of unclaimed hearts?
A sad place surely!
I will keep my heart close to me now
It is too precious to lose and
Your patience may not be endless after all

He had a child perched on his shoulders
I fell in love and married that vision
Little knowing that not so far into the future
God would sit me on His.

Such a love is between equals
Can I accept this match and
take my place at Your side
Say 'My Baba' firmly from the heart
And tie you strongly with a rope of love
that cannot be broken

Such a transforming kind of love
I must ignite the same intensity
of fire that burns the bodies
at the cremation ground
And finish all my impurities

Your love is a lighthouse
Protecting against pitfalls
Leading me forward
Your hand is on my life
So much love.

Places

Poignancy of places
Moments in time
Personal impressions
Painted on my heart's canvas

A sequence of mental snapshots
evoking the memory
of precious days
spent in special places

Sounds and scenes and solitude
Experiences savoured
Stamped on my memory
Sweetly held
Sometimes referred to
Reference points for progress

Madhuban

Madhuban, my Madhuban
"No words can express"
A phrase I found amusing
Now find myself using

What fortune to have my holidays here
Rather than some superficial tourist spot
Spend my carefully saved up days
In this beautiful, highest place of all

I slip into my early morning pattern
Like well-worn and familiar shoes
Awaken early in the morning
For these hours are precious
Pulled by the Father
To leave the warmth of bed
For a more unlimited cocoon

What mystery and magic will unfold
If I rise early, so easy here
And sit in this most powerful and protected
space with You

The night sky black with multitude of stars
Watchman grouped around the fire
I'm somewhat surprised to see
a game of badminton at three

I linger often by the Tower of Peace
Place of sanctuary
Protected on all sides
Honoured as the place
Where our Founder's ashes lie
A memorial to his extraordinary
Life and legacy

Cool, clean marble
Lovingly cared for
Mysterious in the early morning
Brilliant in the midday sun
Beacon in the night's darkness
This sacred spot beckons to me
Brings me instantly into silence

Baba's hut, reflective place
Centred in a sea of greenery
Streams of letters written in red
Cherished by the recipients
Persistent, patient, Father, Guide

18th January approaches
The Seniors' lovingly recounted recollections
Bring Brahma Baba vividly alive
Allow me entry into that close and loving world

Makes me remember the comfort and reassurance
I have experienced
leaning against my father's knees
Safe, protected, most of all loved

The Day of Remembrance
So meticulously prepared for
Both physically and spiritually
Dedicated servers from Calcutta
working through the night
Intricate and wonderful flower creations
Fragrance of roses hanging in the air

Each moment a jewel
Profound silence and brilliant sunshine
Grouped around the Tower of Peace
Dadis, seniors and the guests
In dignified procession.

Coconut, dates and carrot milk
My very favourite breakfast

Baba's cool pristine room
Welcome refuge from the sunshine's glare
and friendly courtyard chatter
I love this place
Am reminded once again of my fortune

I am soothed by the simplicity
and depth of silence
Powerful yet gently reassuring
As he was
Barely anything for himself
Everything for the world

Sunset outing to Baba's rock
Climbing in the footsteps
of those foundation souls
Vast sky and plains meet
My mind soars like an eagle

Senses merge with the setting sun
And peace sinks into my being

It's time to leave
my beloved Madhuban
Sadness and happiness mixed in tears
Final blessings, goodbye drishti
So much sweetness
Truly the Forest of Honey
Total disinterest, unlimited love.

Casa Sangam

Casa Sangam, land of Sunflowers
Oasis of stillness, place to rest
Myriad of meetings, souls converging
Casa Sangam, you're the best

Casa Sangam, land of sweetness
Forged with silence, a deeper bond
Abundantly serving mind and body
Self discovery – fertile ground

Cedar soldiers, standing tall
Some fat, some thin
Some spruce, some need a trim
Guarding, protecting, marking boundaries
Reminds me of our Maryadas

Early morning mist like Madhuban
Subtle blanket on the hills
Wending our way to amrit vela
Welcome lights and flasks to fill

Never seen so many sunflowers
Cheerful faces to the sun
Crowds of sweetcorn
Rows of saplings
Honest effort, kingdom won

Fields of careful cultivation
Herbs and flowers growing wild
Blending together
Each bountiful and beautiful

In its own right
Like this beloved family

Fragrant lavender in profusion
Hum of insects in the air
Daily tasks lovingly executed
Fragrance of virtue, sense of care

Lizards darting everywhere
Startling reminder
of a mind left unattended

Intellect drawn to strong, plain buildings
High beamed ceilings, white washed walls
Shuttered windows, safety, coolness
Mind protected, open to inspiration.

Cool feet dangling in the lake
Peace ripples outwards
and floats back to me

I ask a question in the stillness
Carried on the breeze it comes
'You belong in My heart'

Few adventurous forays
into field and forest
Scratches on my feet as proof
Finding always bright, white pathways
Stretching surely back to home

Sunflowers from my window
Sunflowers everywhere
Some seeds escape an oily future
Falling far in foreign fields
We are likewise, dispersed by destiny
Focus of brightness, forming a family

Settled, stable simple life
Stability serves as a shelter
Allows many things to flourish

Oddly incongruous Casa Sangam
Traffic control music in the wind
Private-public like our living
People peering curiously in
Nothing physical separates us
Invisible wall of purity protects us

Sunflower gold
And cornflower blue
Casa Sangam
I love you.

Global Retreat Centre

A haven of peace and beauty
of power and healing
Fragrant flowers in natural display
Gracing rooms already gracious
A royal place
Serving the present, signalling the future

Peace welcomes you on arrival
Combining with the warmth of smiles
To make a powerful concoction
Melting the stoniest of hearts

Each time I reach here
I marvel afresh
at the wonder of God
and my own fortune

This time particularly
A chance for quiet reflection
Thoughts threading through my mind
As delicately as weave
on tapestry

Treading softly through the grass
Slipping between the trees
The many shades of green
symbolising the growth that flourishes
when there's freedom from attachment

Nature matches my mood
Soft breeze smoothing my face
As Baba's light hand does
sometimes, in meditation

I review my Brahmin life
Feel immensely grateful to Baba
For rescuing me from a boring middle age
Restoring the pure child and
guiding me towards mastery

I treasure coming here so much
Gracious GRC
Thank you Dadi for your vision
Thank you Baba for your love.

My Spiritual Teachers

I feel so much love and regard for these Dadis, extraordinary women whose balance of authority and humility commands my respect but welcomes me into closeness. These teachers are physically present in my life whereas the relationship with the two Babas and Mama is more subtle, yet as real and influential as I wish it to be. Their unlimited wisdom and pure love has restored my belief in myself as valuable and evoked my inner strength and security. They all continue to guide and support me on this journey of self-awareness. Last but not least is Vishnu, symbolically present, who stands behind my other teachers and in front of me. Vishnu holds for me a vision of a future world of peace and happiness and the spiritual means to manifest it.

To Baba

You are everyone's imaginings
Yet uniquely, concisely Yourself
An eternal, indivisible point
You are light out of darkness

You are the Lord of Light
Challenging now the Prince of Darkness
For the soul's light, though never extinguished
has allowed the darkness to dominate
And has neither the knowledge nor the strength
to renew itself

It is the closing of the day, or rather night
And You have come to take us back
For most being dry and tired of stumbling
Are longing for the peace of home

There are always hero parts in human history
Special moments, special souls
Whose qualities and destiny moves them
to weave a different thread
In the fabric of world events

It's such a moment now
Though this unique movement
works a deeper, stronger thread
Against the common weave
Creating a new, though subtle colour
Passing almost unnoticed in an age
Where little goes unreported

I am remembering odd verses from a Christian song
Interesting how certain things resonate and remain
with you
'Dance, dance wherever you may be
For I am the Lord of the Dance, said he
And I'll find you all, wherever you may be
And I'll lead you all in the Dance, said he'

At different moments in far-flung places
A chord is struck
Another dancer joins the dance
Each mastering the steps
At a different pace
In a separate space

You collected me in this strange manner
A school gymnasium seeming an unlikely place
to meet with God
And I was unaware even that I was searching

But You called me and I came
Blissfully unaware of what lay ahead
Tears and transformation, bliss and battles
Ignorance was for me a safety
Otherwise I might have chosen
to languish where I was
Making the best of a bad job
Endlessly smoothing over and sustaining
an illusion of happiness

You are threaded eternally
in love and duty to all souls
But ours is a special claim
on your attention
Requiring as it does an unusual tenancy
to carry out this unique task
For which all souls remember You

You are the Mother and the Father
A title only Bharat knows
And as a mother in this birth
I am intrigued to watch
Your role of Mother
Played out in different ways and forms

You are the Ocean, always full
And yet You empty Yourself for us
So all our emptiness can be removed
And filling up, can nourish others
With your wisdom, power and love

You are constantly full and overflowing
Like Bharat in its Golden Age
Bharat the golden sparrow
The land which holds the memorials of Your birth

You know the secrets of my heart
Yet wait for me to tell

Master of a process
That I must learn as well

I am Your child
But You are also mine
Who else but us could claim
this odd relationship with the Almighty

How to fulfil a love like this
For it holds a high demand
A special sort of responsibility
which stretches on and on
But draws a high return

I will never leave You
For You have invested much in me
and I in You
And You have promised not to
leave us till the end
And I to You am tied

in the sweetest of all bondages
Annually renewed

You are the silence and the sweetness
The laughter and the love
The firmness out of kindness
Most powerful force for good

It's time for the pattern of events
to move further forward
Fulfilling Brahma's subtle but unlimited vision
of a world family

And change again the pattern must
For time is calling
Your revelation waits
And we must call the time.

Brahma Baba

Hero actor, hero part
Arjuna and Adi Dev
Your memorial, also ours, is here
Living and non-living neighbours

So clean and straight and tall
High intelligent forehead
Destiny written there
Simple life-style, simple dress
Outer appearance mirroring inner quality

84 births' worth of experience
Processed and becoming pure
Makes you a rich resource for us
A worldly wise adviser

No childish guru or remote recluse
For you and life have touched and touched again
Your eyes see deep inside the soul
And far into the future

Discerning master jeweller
First of diamonds
Later jewels of a different kind
Your skill in crafting finest pieces
Shifting focus to creating character

Successful, wealthy businessman
Surrendering everything
to do a deal with God
Earning a truer, longer lasting income
Inspiring others to do the same

Austere in a totally love-filled way
Accepting nothing but essentials for yourself
Money that has never been your master
Now sustaining a new and growing family

Amazing knowledge unfolding in your head
A special, secret blueprint
Minutely detailed
Painstakingly revealed

Line drawings in the beginning
Outline sketches
Detail building slowly
Colour forming
Until the picture is complete

Did you have to deeply dig and dig
Or was it all just there
Layer upon layer
Rising to the surface

Shiv Baba's seed of thought
Triggering your memory
Fertilising feelings long lain dormant
Unique and special soul
Eternally selected to hold the archive
of this hidden history

Brahma, Vishnu, Vishnu Brahma
Eternally, endlessly connected
One born from the other
With Krishna dancing in between

Manners maketh Man
So true for you
A king in all your births
Royalty and reality
Accessible to all, irrespective of age and status
The basis – true humility and total self-respect

Balanced, whole and integrated personality
A purity so complete that it transforms
the elements of your body by the end
Soft, transparent, feather-light

You left a legacy in the Dadis
A memorial in the Tower of Peace
Your thought created all of us
Your love sustains us still.

Mama

Dear Mama, I wasn't with you physically
Here on this mountain top
Yet still I know you and sense that you know me
Feel you are the mother of all my lives
The model for the mother in me

You became Mama in a matter of moments
An astonishing metamorphosis from
bright and brilliant butterfly to
subtle, silent angel

Seemingly in a second
You surrendered your jewellery,
clothes and intellect
Catching instead more precious, priceless jewels
And a golden path stretching into the future

Baba placed the urn of knowledge on your head
And it became a cooking pot to feed the
whole family
You ground the ingredients of that truth
And mindful of our weaker digestive systems
Fed it to us in a form we could absorb

You were always full and always free
And so were able to satisfy all of us
And when the pot was almost empty
Your faith and courage held us firm

For when God is present
There are always miracles
And a mother's honour
Has to be maintained

Brahma carried God and you carried us
Holding together such a vast and disparate family
Teaching us the principles of economy and order
Cleanliness of the body, mind and heart

We felt that you belonged to each of us
Knowing you belonged only to One
Your love shone from your eyes
Keeping us refreshed, taking us beyond

Yet it was not a soft love
But a love that nourished our bones
And made us strong

You were so clean and clear and light inside
That you could carry the physical pain
Without it showing on your face

Saving us from that particular sorrow
Sustaining us until the end

No ending really, just a change of form
Your household is immensely greater now
Caring for us without us knowing it
Providing what is needed
Whether money, hands or healing

Your brilliance has sparked another human form
But the greater part of you is in the world of light
Touching all our lives,
smoothing away our worries
Gently but firmly pulling us
towards our destination.

Dadi Kumarka

I've watched you in the morning
In the pristine cleanliness of your room
And marvelled at your composure
Your calmness, light and grace

You seem not to mind
this early morning intrusion
But smile and nod in that special way of yours
And feed us titbits from that day's murli

You and that room sit in my memory
Simplicity and brilliance combined
Ordinary actions transformed
by your presence and royalty

I come not out of adulation or devotion
But from a pure wish to watch your face
As you might have watched Brahma Baba's
Just soaking in the brightness and strength
And a warm feeling of being folded into the family

You are extraordinarily beautiful in a way
that is ocean's apart from worldly convention
The stamp of an emperor is already etched
on your features and in your bearing
Compelling eyes in that lion's face
reflect a magic blend of power and purity

I could so easily feel distant and in awe of you
A strange child from another land
But your immense authority is matched
by a love and humility which bridges that distance

So, not understanding the words,
I catch the vibration
Feel at home in your vision and in your heart

You have made Madhuban belong to all of us
From there you send us messages of care
and caution
Enquiring after our health and wellbeing
and the state of our hearts

You have this special ability to bring people close
And to maintain that precious unity
Children from all corners of the world
Welded into one
You carry the responsibility for world service
Yet it sits so lightly on your shoulders

You carry it as easily as a child with a ball
Just a plaything in a game played with God

Yours is such an indomitable spirit
Not for you the months of careful convalescence
But with Baba as your nursing companion
You wing your way here to be with
your far-flung children

We know we cannot hold you
For you belong only to God
But we can hold you in our hearts
For your vision makes us tall
Young saplings growing into tall trees
that will empower and nurture others
As you so consistently encourage and sustain us

Dadi - we love you.

Dadi Gulzar

I would like to be as silent as you
No wasteful or superfluous words
Moving so smoothly from total involvement
to introversion and back again

There is a plainness and simplicity about you
Like a country woman
deeply rooted in what you know
A rich household of experience within you

I love you for your accessibility and remoteness
Your presence carries a silence that defies
interruption
But you are always so patient with us
Giving so generously of your accumulated wisdom
and experience
But never tempted into irrelevance

You share so much, as all the Dadis do
According to your different personalities
I love to watch you all together
Such interconnectedness and co-operation
Yet so uniquely individual

Have you always been so silent?
So economical with your words
No childish exuberance for you perhaps
Destiny's line already visible
To easily reach and recognise God

Yours is such a special role
Coming and going to the subtle region
As one room to another
Carrier of questions, conveyor of replies
Faithful reporter of those subtle scenes

You will not be hurried
There is a carefulness about you
that is nothing to do with selfishness
But all about mindfulness

You are such a private person
Perhaps it's your particular relationship
to BapDada
For whom you prepare so carefully
As if making a room ready
Down to the tiniest detail
For a very special guest

I'm still a little in awe of you
But deeply value our occasional encounters
A few precious, quality days in Scotland
Taking every opportunity for your company
Your amazing drishti drawing me down
into an endless well of silence

Or sitting studying by the Tower of Peace
You passed me walking
And that moment's interaction
Added extra brightness to a place already brilliant

But what stands out for me
Is that Delhi evening shopping trip
One of those odd scenes in the drama
When someone says "come"
And you respond like a child to an
unexpected treat

New as I was to this brahmin life
My mind awash with images and experiences
I found it hard to reconcile my fresh memory
Of your chariot form
With that mundane purchase of a dozen towels

Recalling the strangeness of that scene now
I realise it encapsulates this path for me

The ordinary and extraordinary
Mundane and magical
Constantly mixing together

You are so beautiful
Seeing you, we see Bapdada
But we love you for yourself
Welcome, welcome from our hearts.

Dadi Janki

How to write of you
Courageous child of Baba
Cheerful Commander of
His Western army

Almost too close
For me to be dispassionate
Your presence elicits
a range of emotion
From devotion to extreme discomfort
Indifference is not a possibility

Forged in that original furnace
Made of stronger stuff than us
Your love is more a father's than a mother's
The ease of our relationship
dependent totally on my self-respect

You hold the highest standards
constantly in front of us
Treading sometimes on our sensitivities
No compromise with you

And would we really have it otherwise
Accepting for ourselves a lesser inheritance
You are not our creation anyway
To fashion, fix and change

Adaptable, enduring visionary
How else could you have flowered
so brilliantly and persistently
in this damp and often chilly
corner of the West.

Propelling Baba's vision forward
No limits to your universe
From early days in cramped, small rooms
to stately homes and House of Lords
Vision taking shape before our eyes
Who knows what's next!

Boredom is not a word in your vocabulary
Your energy and timetable easily outstripping ours
No-one dare ask you how you are
For periodic illness of the body
seems just an opportunity for settlement
and service on a higher plane

Your intellect is fathoms deep
Often unfathomable to me
Diving deep, divining always
the freshest food for own and others' sustenance

Knowledge flows from you unceasingly
Ocean, river, lake combined
Stable mind and fine-tuned intellect
Totally aligned with God

Challenging, surprising and inspiring
Master of essence and elaboration
Intuitively gauging the mood of the gathering
You shift and change from ocean's depths
to light and humorous dialogue

Endless queues outside your door
Super spiritual social worker
Attention total, straight forgotten
Return to silence in a second

Diminutive, wet-haired Thursday's child
Hearts meet and melt in nectar's sweetness
Your love for God and hopes in us
are unmistakable

Your mind and Baba's meet
Few jewelled words emerge
Resonating deeply
Constantly repeating
How to thank you
Baba's Janak
Our DJ.

The Vishnu Effect

Mysterious, magical Vishnu
Magnificently arrayed
Simplicity and silence seated side by side
Each minute aspect
Filled with meaning
Awakening our memories

Shiva's dance of creation and destruction
Vishnu shimmering in between
Accessible only to those
whose past and future meet
In recognition of the Master

Pictures passing before his eyes
Imprinting their message
Divinely inspired by the Supreme Director
Deeply informing our future

Uniquely selected, seasoned urn
Immune to any onslaught
Able to hold the whole
From exquisitely beautiful
To bitter in the extreme

Future new world clearly visible to the Father
Why remember that which is to be destroyed

Fearless, intrepid traveller
Forging the path for us to follow
Forever focussing our attention
On the One Father
Filling us with faith

Swift yet subtle arrow
Pierced the armour of my indifference

A love to die for
Hit home to the heart of my longing
Creation of virtue
Destruction of weakness
Vishnu behind and in between
Symbols of method and accomplishment
Present effort and future reward

Three forms or is it four
Symbolic, subtle secrets
Moving into reality
Rhythmically threading
Through all our lives

Vivid, vibrant personality
Strength and stability
Standing in the midst of the family
Encompassing everyone
Canopy of protection

Sheltering, sustaining us
Even today

We have to follow the Father
In all four subjects
This is the method
For becoming complete

Vishnu – He is this and so are we
Blueprint of a family path
Whose ever-changing form
Endures for all the cycle

You are the rich presence in my room
Bridging, balancing, bringing together
the scattered elements of my being
Providing purpose, restoring wholeness

Remembrance of that love remains
Hope and happiness held in you
Has stayed with me always.

Occasions

This first poem, the only one to rhyme,
remains my favourite. The more so because
it marked the beginning of a creative journey
which has given me, and I hope others, so
much joy and faith in myself and God.
There are many occasions worth marking.
This is a small selection of poems about
significant events, some of which I was
asked to write and others which I felt
drawn to write.

Mother's Day

Today is Mother's Day
So I would like to say
That mothering isn't just a role
But more a quality of the soul
And all of you can mothers be
If it's a need that you can see

It's love and care and nourishment
And cakes and kindness freely sent
A watchful eye, a listening ear
A hug of warmth to lessen fear
A smoothing out, a gentle hand
A love that's constant and unbound

Endurance, strength and cups of tea
And sticking plaster for your knee

Love filled hopes and tirelessness
And clearing up of endless mess
Knowing when it's time for bed
Arranging things inside your head

And up and down and in and out
And wipe your feet and please don't shout
Cos Dad's asleep!
And laughs and tears are motherhood
Hope it's now like brotherhood
And pain and sorrow in the life
Especially when attachment's rife

I loved them when they were little
And I love them now they're tall
Perhaps I shouldn't say it

But I'm going to after all
Especially since God found me
And taught me how to be
To love and love and love a lot
Yet know how to be free

And all of you can mothers be
If it's a need that you can see
And now the world's my family
And anyway it's scones for tea.

For the Queen's Golden Jubilee

I remember clearly your Coronation
I was five and you were 25
No school that day
But parties in the streets
And waving flags and coronation mugs

Few had tellies in those days
But we had one
So all the neighbours came to watch
at our house

Rich pageantry, royal celebration
Your people embraced you and the occasion
with extra exuberance
Welcome contrast to post-war dullness
New era dawning
More joyful cause for community togetherness

Young Elizabeth, not long married
Thrust dramatically
Into the forefront of public life
What must it have felt like
Hearing the news from a distant land
Beloved father's leaving
Your sudden call to duty

But you were trained as he was not
Destiny having wrested
both of you
from quieter background
gentler seclusion

Beautiful, brave Elizabeth
Strong sense of duty
Slender shoulders squaring
to accept this greater responsibility

You had already won a place
In people's hearts

You and Margaret
Reared in a loving family
Kind and caring girls
Lovers of animals
Committed contribution in years of war

Song created in your honour
In a golden court
There's a heart of gold
That belongs to you and me
The sweetest Queen
The world has seen
Wearing a golden crown

Royal, red road to Buckingham Palace
The changing of the Guard
Times have surely changed
But not your sense of duty
Stable in crisis
Surrendered to service

Inspiring others to do the same
Qualities of respect and honour
Faith and strength and fortitude

Responsible, well-informed Elizabeth
Daily duty dealt with care
Determination to see things through
Private suffering, public face of dignity

Loyal, lovely Lilibet
Detached observer
of the changing face
of family, nation, Commonwealth

Domain diminishing
Your wisdom showing
in letting go of that
which cannot be retained
But holding on to
higher values

You ride in state
Through the palace gate
Beauty the whole world can see
Not of matching coat and hat
But deepest dignity.

Peace of Mind Retreat

Precious, priceless
Peace of Mind
Hearts engaging
Minds retracing
Time to listen
Silent space

Arduous journey
Soon receding
Tiredness seeping
Strangers meeting
Agendas leaving
Openness to change

Walks in silence
Starlit skies
Listening, learning
Reflecting, sharing

Warmth and welcome
Soothe the soul

Part of a gathering
Sense of belonging
Acknowledging differences
Not all plain sailing
Barriers dissolving
Vibrations of love

Mind like a child
Nurture it well
Likes to be free
But not running wild
Face full of sunshine
Peaceful inside
Choices and challenges
Achievements recounted
Unique expression
Connecting threads

Tao of the Traveller
We watch and wonder
Stories and dances
And sacred songs

Sifting thoughts
In silvery silence
Time to ponder
Chance to dream
Dadi's wisdom, Dadi's drishti
Family closeness and toli

Lake of knowledge
Dipping, diving
Rich memories storing
Time is calling
French fries fragrance
Loveful leaving
Anything missing
More ice cream please.

Diwali Celebration

Brilliant Retreat Centre
Dadi's presence
Deepaks twinkling
Happy Diwali

Warmth and welcome
Royal gathering
Joyful meeting
of age-old friends

Living lamps
and lively laughter
Lifting spirits
Spreading light
These chandeliers
are our memorial
Threaded together
Sparkling tonight

Beautiful Baba
You have ignited
the lamp of hope
in all our hearts

We have cleaned out
the cupboards of our
minds and hearts
Putting in place
the treasures of the spirit

Remembering Shiv Baba
Shivalaya is not far away
Golden glimpses of the future
Health and wealth and harmony
Future kingdom reflected here
Purity, strength and royalty
Greetings and congratulations
Oceans of gratitude to GRC.

To Diamond House

Seed of India, sown in England
Flourishing now in fullest bloom
Precious earth from every continent
Forecast of a future
Encompassing the world

Out of a chrysalis of intense activity
Obstacles encountered on the way
Concrete proof that faith brings victory
Combined with highest guarantee

We have grown with you, Diamond House
Not without some small discomfort

Expanding our capacity along with yours
Child of beauty born before our eyes
Unveiled in airy, spacious splendour
Final polishing yet to do

Striking presence, in sympathy with surroundings
Commitment to quality, Jewel in the Crown

Dignified, distinguished Diamond House
Royal Message of Respect
Acknowledging spiritual contribution
Fostering harmony, valuing faith

Colours of creamy sunshine
Calm and cooling greens and blues
Silence laid between the layers
Conducive to quietness, atmosphere of peace

You are not a twin to Global House
Much more a complementary partner

Extending hospitality, conference facility
Centre of learning, creating our lives

Three Dadis dear to all our hearts
Entwined together, each unique
Bestowing their particular blessing
Enthusiasm, respect, a trustee life

Lines of love link us to Madhuban
Source and resource of so much strength
Wise, benevolent eyes watch over us
Angels gathering, Jewel of Light

Diamond denotes the highest value
Rainbow of colours contained in light
Beauty of virtues, hidden facets
Shining outwards, beacon for the world
New hope, new scope
Unlimited horizons
Two structures built on One support
Magic of love and co-operation
Sparkle of success in Diamond Lane.

A New Millennium

Somewhere in my head
The news is being read
News not of the past or present
But of the future

Storm clouds gather overhead
Fragments of our world
Breaking apart and coming together.
Inside our minds and hearts
A mixture of anxiety and anticipation
Foreboding and faith

Too often I am anchored to the ground
Dealing with mundane, often petty concerns
Weighed down by the world's woes.

Can I be farsighted like an eagle
Soaring in my imagination
Widening my vision into the unlimited

As surely as dawn comes after night
Now rests the certainty in my head
That the world's day lies ahead
Glimmering in the distance.
Omens of Jupiter replacing those of Saturn
Health and harmony healing
The present day's unease

Let me see the future through your eyes
Far sighted visionary
In whom the light of God sits.

Let me stand alongside you
And look into the future
Clearly visible in your gaze
Precious pieces of a timeless jigsaw
Blueprint of a perfect world.

Forms coming together to form a perfect pattern
Human Beings touching but only lightly
Treading softly on an abundant earth
Deeply loving but not intruding
on each other's lives.

It's time for vision
Time for change.
Standing on the threshold
of a new millennium.

Celebrating Lives

A time to move on
Opportunity for healing
Mood of reflection
Appreciation of quality
Mixture of feelings
Openly accepted
A chance to celebrate a life

Naturally Naoise

What's new for Naoise now?
God knows, drama knows
A future firmly fixed in happiness
A place forever in the family

Singer of songs
So much sweetness
Dreaming dancer
In harmony with humanity

Forthright, straight and honest Naoise
Never judging, always accepting
Touching the child in everyone
Fostering the love
But underlining the leader

Expansive, open-minded soul
Living as you chose to do
Always your own person
Big River, meeting the Ocean
Lovely, exuberant child of God

Tireless, dedicated server
Prison pioneer, a powerful precedent
Sustaining that creation
Inspiring others to move it forward

Within the suffering of the body
Giving still with so much love and lightness
Entertaining always
Defying deadlines
Driven by the desire to serve

Laughter, love and chips for tea
Endlessly surprising
Limits stretching
Wheelchair flying on the Heath

Forgetting nothing
Forever remembering
Picture of pansies, precious family
Imperfect, perfect Naoise

Boundless love no longer containable
In such a narrowed form
Leaping forward now to sparkle
in a more favourable setting

Compassionate, courageous Naoise
Holding your kingly dignity until the last
Seeing us celebrate
You surrendered softly and slipped away

Lingering taste of joy and chocolate cake
No need for tears
Though tears allowed
Treasuring a life lived fully
Leaving for us a legacy of love.

Loving Louise

How to remember you
Niece of mine
Hardly knew you
Never took the time

Early glimpses recollected
Pretty, curly headed child
Gawky, awkward leggy youngster
Sensitive, quick to take offence
Self conscious, stubborn, insecure
Needing love and reassurance

Prickly, protective outer casing
Glowing chestnut, hidden fruit
Who could predict your later flowering
Important personal victories

The Cotswolds called you
Famous for antiques
Choosing now for sleepy quaintness
Still at heart a Yorkshire lass

New found interest, budding passion
Love for solid English Oak
Perceptive eye for original treasures
Restoring them with craft and care

Moving into independence
Supported still by closest bond
Shy, reserved, a private person
Slow to trust but loyal friend

Practical prowess, romantic dreamer
Who can know the truth of Lou
Strands of memories, interwoven
mother, father, brother, friend

Dark times to deal with
Determination to see things through
Comfort curling up with cats
Courage, strength, tenacity

Fun and laughter, new relationship
Work and play and interests shared
Alliance of loners, understanding deepening
Nurtured by a respect for space

I have not witnessed your transformation
Hear it now from others lips
Like a butterfly emerging
Oddly beautiful, vulnerable still

Louise relinquished, spirit soaring
Constrained no more by form or fears
Peace and love are now your partners
Fiddle music following you.

Just Jeff

Early morning rising
Beckoning greens
Feeling of freedom
A chance to dream

Exercise, air and open spaces
Comfortable companionship
Challenging handicap
Undaunted, undefeated drive

Stoical, seemingly stubborn Jeffrey
Stiff exterior, soft-centered sweetness
Hidden world of thoughts and feelings
Touchingly revealed through the written word

Clever, somehow frustrated intellect
Early ambition, couldn't sustain

Concealed disappointments
Danger of dogmatism
Avid reader, interested in the world

Handsome, dignified and distinguished
Strength and courage, Yorkshire grit
Father's pride not easily communicated
A sense of humour dryly dealt

Watcher and player
Sport your passion
As disability demanded
the court be relinquished
Dedicated secretary of fixtures emerged

Never a moaner
Positive and persevering

Distress of the body diminished
But never destroyed your spirit

Armchair world, a restful refuge
Haven for babies, reliable lap
Sums and stories
Gentle grandfather
Comfortable arms to rest and play

Legacy of letters
Lovingly written
Lines of relationship
Sealed and secure

Pain is settled
Peace prevails
A path of green and gold
Stretches before you.

Brendan

Bidding farewell to Brendan
France destined to witness
your departure from the body
The soul unfettered flies

Practical, very private person
Protecting others from your pain
Concerned and caring, work mates' mentor
Gentle nature, generous heart

Responsible eldest brother
Loved and loving father
Finding forgiveness
All relationships restored

Warm and weathered face
Lifetime of physical work
Wiry, weary body
No longer willing to restrict
your resilient spirit

Cheerful, courageous Brendan
Determination defying difficulties
Youthfulness of spirit, natural purity
Your smile and sweetness
Leave with us a lasting legacy

Pain has left you
Peace remains
Inner strength awakened
Carries you forward
To a sun-filled, smiling future.

Spencer

Sweet, sweet Spencer
Short but significant
time spent together
The gift you gave us
far outweighed your tiny form
Freeing you to fly
Holding you in our hearts
Safe journey Spencer
Super hero
Sweet Spencer sweet.

Virtue

It lies inside each of us
Clean and pure
Like an underground spring
Untapped for aeons
Buried under a brittle surface
Layers deep
Resting, waiting
to be freed
A laser beam of light
penetrates
Love, pure and powerful
Pierces the layers of illusion
Skilful Surgeon's hand
Totally dedicated
Absolutely benevolent
Virtue emerges
to herald and sustain
A long awaited golden day.

Silence

Silence steals humbly over the world
Shifting thoughts, simplifying lives
Strengthening purpose and stirring
Long-unfulfilled hopes and dreams

Sitting in this quiet space
I saunter through the many
avenues of my mind
Observing things done well and badly
Surveying future plans
In the vast sea of possibilities

The silence settles gently
Enfolding me softly
Like a cloak
Smooth and silky to the touch

Silence edges into my mind
Silver tendrils weaving
Subtle threads of thought
Lifting me away
from mundane matters

Silence, once synonymous with fear
Becoming now my comforter,
friend and guide
Silence, once empty save for enemies
Now a rich repository of treasures

I begin a love affair with silence
Sensing somehow
That to love silence
Is to love myself.

Divine Vision

What is reality
How much can I see
Depends on the vision
That's given to me

Life's a kaleidoscope
of colour and sound
Feelings and actions
Familiar ground

Caught in the turbulence
Thoughts tossed in the waves
Hardly notice surroundings
Let alone my own face

Pulled out of the whirlpool
Impelled to be still

I'm catching a current
Feel a strange sort of thrill

A landscape is opening
A history unfolds
A silvery secret
Repeatedly told

Emerging inside me
A crystal clear thought
Of a world that awaits us
A destiny caught

Thank you my Father
Beloved and Child
For You hold the key
And Your love
Holds my mind.

Purity

Purity is precious
Purity is me
I come from a place of purity
It's where I want to be

I didn't think about it
Until You spoke to me
Then I knew I loved it
Had always been part of me

Purity is childhood
A chance to be carefree
Purity is innocence
But not naivety

More than just the body
It's the essence of the soul

Keeps my vision crystal clear
Draws all things back to whole

Purity breaks down barriers
Allows my love to flow
Purity's my protection
Enables me to grow

It's the basis of my happiness
The basis of my peace
The energy of the universe
It's freedom and release

I've made a pledge of purity
Renewed it every year
Simple, sweet and sacred bond
A sign of royalty.

Peace

Sincerely have I searched for you
Sadly have I lamented your loss
Stridently have I petitioned and protested for you
Sweetly have I composed cantatas in your name
Silently have I prayed for you

Fatally have I fought for you
Killed those I thought were your enemies
Only to find you moved further away
Pain not peace prevailed

Peace calls to me softly
Touching a deeply held memory
of a life lived together
Naturally, gently entwined
United as one

Peace is now my private practice
Taking care of my thoughts and feelings
Standing guard over my actions
Restoring my mind to a sanctuary
Where peace can preside
Seeding a world of peace.

To Humility

Born out of introversion
Nourished with simplicity and love
Happiness is your companion
You are the soil in which
self-respect grows and flourishes

You are the opposite of pushy
Need no external show
Seems strange that one so plainly clad
Should wield so great an authority

Magic ingredient in my life
Harmoniser of relationships
You free me from defensive reactions
And the need to comment endlessly
on other people's actions

You train my ears to listen
Bring softness and sweetness to my speech
Help me lose my 'I'ness
Serving always but no subservience

I feel stronger, lighter in your company
More confident, more at ease
You help build tolerance and stability
Open up my mind and heart

You are such a great equaliser
Drawing others close
Empowering their potential
Building bridges, dissolving barriers
Forging connections with the family

Drawing me into quietness
You clothe me in an angel dress
Help me catch the subtle signals
See the beauty everywhere

You whisper 'Whilst alive
you have to learn
to die
to bow'

You are so evident
in both our Babas
The eyes, the words
and the divine activities

Humility my light and lovely friend
You take my hand
And lead me to a place
of Truth and Purity.

Courage

Taking courage into our hands
Hands that cope in crisis
That care and caution
Hands that create the future

Extending our compassion
Holding the world in our heart
Keeping the commitment to carrying through
An instinct to preserve

Moving past the many barriers
Seen and unseen
which block our progress
Becoming who we are in a whole sense

Not driven by competition
But drawn together by a passion
to secure a world
Built on trust.

Silence

Simple and sweet is silence
Yet deep and profound its fruit
Taste the sweetness
Savour the stillness
Sense the unlimited
stretch of space
And sink into its heart.

This Family

So fortunate
To be part of this family
A feeling of safety
A sense of belonging
An open door of welcome
All over the world

This family is a fixture in my life
Don't always appreciate it
Can never leave it
Definitely never dull
Durable as a diamond

Wisely supportive
Sometimes scary
Whatever I see
Reflects back to me

Deep love if not always liking
Its life and mine
Inextricably linked
To stay in its heart
Is to expand my own
Beyond imagining

Boundless love
Sometimes bruising
Am I brave enough to stay on board?
Until this bizarre yet brilliant boat
Reaches the shore

If I sulk with this family
Maya will steal me away
Nor can I compromise
Retain a little of the sannyasi
Find it doesn't fit

With the picture of this future family
So firmly embedded in me

Such an amazing Gardener
To have gathered in
Flowers from all corners
Colours of every hue
Co-existing together
Complementing each other
Still completely individual

Nowhere will I find
Such a Mother and Father
Loving, guiding, forgiving
Feeding me nourishing food
Fostering such growth
that will carry me forward
Into the future

All our rough edges
Rubbing together
Will finally achieve
A finely honed finish
Just like the diamonds
Our Founder used to fashion

In this gathering
So much sweetness
So much love
I am proud to belong
To this pure lineage
Know in my heart
That finally we will fly
Home together.

ABOUT THE
Brahma Kumaris World Spiritual University

The Brahma Kumaris World Spiritual University is an international organisation working at all levels of society for positive change. Established in 1937, the University now has more than 7,000 centres in more than 90 countries. It actively participates in a wide range of educational programmes in areas such as youth, women, men, environment, peace, values, social development, education, health and human rights.

In 1996, the University's Academy for a Better World was opened in Mount Abu, India. The Academy offers individuals from all walks of life opportunities for life-long innovative learning. Residential programmes are centred on human, moral and spiritual values and principles. The University also supports the Global Hospital and Research Centre in Mount Abu, India.

Local centres around the world provide courses and lectures in meditation and positive values, supporting individuals in recognising their own inherent qualities and abilities, and making the most of their lives.

All courses and activities are offered free of charge.

BRAHMA KUMARIS WORLD SPIRITUAL UNIVERSITY

WORLD HEADQUARTERS
Po Box No 2, Mount Abu 307501, Rajasthan, India
Tel: (+91) 2974-238261 to 68   Fax: (+91) 2974-238952
E-mail: bkabu@bkindia.com

**INTERNATIONAL CO-ORDINATING OFFICE &
REGIONAL OFFICE FOR EUROPE AND THE MIDDLE EAST**
Global Co-operation House, 65-69 Pound Lane, London
NW10 2HH, UK
Tel: (+44) 208 727 3350   Fax: (+44) 208 727 3351
E-mail: london@bkwsu.com

REGIONAL OFFICES

AFRICA
Global Museum for a Better World,
Maua Close,
Westlands,
PO Box 123
00606 Nairobi, Kenya
Tel: (+254) 20 374 1849   Fax: (+254) 20 374 3885
E-mail: Nairobi@bkwsu.org

AUSTRALIA AND SOUTH EAST ASIA
78 Alt Street,
Ashfield,
Sydney NSW 2131,
Australia
Tel: (+61) 2 9716 7066   Fax: (+61) 2 9716 7795
E-mail: Sydney@bkwsu.org

THE AMERICAS AND THE CARIBBEAN
Global Harmony House
46 S. Middle Neck Road
Great Neck, NY 11021, USA
Tel: (+1) 516 773 0971   Fax: (+1) 516 773 0976
E-mail: newyork@bkwsu.com

RUSSIA, CIS AND THE BALTIC COUNTRIES
2 Gospitalnaya Ploschad, build. 1
Moscow - 111020, Russia
Tel: (+7) 095 263 02 47   Fax: (+7) 095 261 32 24
E-mail: moscow@bkwsu.org

www.bkwsu.org

www.bkpublications.com
enquiries@bkpublications.com